*The Agile Manager's Guide To*

# GIVING
# GREAT PRESENTATIONS

*The Agile Manager's Guide To*

# GIVING
# GREAT PRESENTATIONS

By Jeff Olson

*Velocity Business Publishing*
*Bristol, Vermont USA*

*For Louisa*

**Copyright © 1997 by Velocity Business Publishing, Inc.**
**All Rights Reserved**
**Printed in the United States of America**
**Library of Congress Catalog Card Number 97-90829**
**ISBN 0-9659193-1-5**
**Design by Andrea Gray**
**Title page illustration by Elayne Sears**

If you'd like additional copies of this book or a catalog of books in the Agile Manager Series™, get in touch with us.

- **Write us at:**
  Velocity Business Publishing, Inc.
  15 Main Street
  Bristol, VT 05443 USA

- **Call us at:**
  1-888-805-8600 in North America (toll-free)
  1-802-453-6669 from all other countries

- **Fax us at:**
  1-802-453-2164

- **E-mail us at:**
  info@agilemanager.com

- **Visit our Web site at:**
  http://www.agilemanager.com

Call or write for a free, timesaving "extra-fast" edition of this book—or visit www.agilemanager.com/special.htm.

# Contents

**Other Books in the Agile Manager Series™:**

# Introduction

Does the thought of speaking in front of a group make your heart flutter and turn your hands clammy?

The good news: You can get over that fear in a matter of weeks if not days (and sometimes hours). Even better news: Good public speaking and presentation skills can do more for your career than years of experience and an arm-load of degrees from the most prestigious universities. That's how much business people respect and admire those who can educate an audience or move it to action.

Why are good presentation skills more important than ever? The business world is changing. Teamwork is in vogue, companies are "flattening" out as traditional hierarchies disappear, and partnerships and alliances with organizations outside your own are becoming more common. Even senior managers have less opportunity to "command and control" a body of troops—yet they have more responsibility than ever to motivate people to act in line with the organization's strategies and values.

Good speaking skills can be learned. As Dale Carnegie often said, "No one is a born speaker." To learn, you need this book.

You also need opportunities to speak in front of others. If you don't have such opportunities often enough, you can create them by taking a Dale Carnegie course or joining Toastmasters.

You'll never regret acquiring presentation skills. For one thing, a majority of Americans, according to the *Book of Lists*, would rather die (literally) than get up to speak in front of an audience. If you are among this group, imagine the personal power you will earn by confronting one of your deepest fears and overcoming it.

For another, presentation skills go a long way in business. The opportunities to inform, influence, and get action from a large number of people are increasing, even for employees at the bottom of the organization chart. And the ability to write isn't enough in today's business world. Powerful speaking beats a good memo any day. It's also a magnet that draws attention to you and your abilities.

In short, speaking skills in business are a strong component of leadership—the ability to define the future and get people to march into it with you.

This book outlines the basics of speaking and presentation skills. It's designed to give you the maximum number of tools in the briefest amount of space. There's no fluff or filler—you can read it in one or two sittings, and then keep it nearby to refer to again and again.

Let's begin.

# Organizing and Preparing Your Talk

*"Don't spend ten minutes or ten hours preparing your talk: Spend ten weeks or ten months. Better still, spend ten years."*

DALE CARNEGIE

*Chapter One*

# $B$efore You Begin . . .

The Agile Manager picked up the phone. The boss.

"Howdy," said the boss in his Texas twang. "Here's what I need you to do. On Thursday I'm supposed to go before the board to outline the new product line. It's supposed to be a purely informational presentation, but the CEO said many of the board members are skeptical. He said he'd 'appreciate' it—nice word for an order, eh?—if I did my best to convince them this is the right thing to do.

"Here's the problem: I can't be there on Thursday, and the meeting can't be put off. You're the only one I trust to take my place. I talked to the CEO about having you stand in, and he said that was fine as long as I believed in you. I do. You know the project and the reasons behind it as well as I. Well?"

"Sure, I'd love to do it," said the Agile Manager.

"Great," said the boss. "4:30 in the conference room. Do I need to tell you how important this is?"

"Nope." The Agile manager hung up and gulped. He tried to think of a more important presentation he'd ever given. He couldn't think of one. But then again, he didn't know of a project—the new product line—he'd ever given more of himself to, either. He'd do fine—as long as he prepared.

*"Heigh-ho, heigh-ho" he began to sing as he pulled out a fresh sheet of paper to outline the talk.*

Someone has asked you to say a few words to a group of people. Fantastic—here's an opportunity to make a difference to your organization. It's also an opportunity to shine in front of co-workers, or perhaps your boss and the boss's boss. But before you agree to speak, do some hard thinking.

### Know Your Subject

The first thing to ask yourself is, "Am I qualified to speak on this topic?" Unless the answer is a resounding yes, don't waste your time or anybody else's. Your lack of knowledge will show, together with a lack of confidence. And you won't have any of the enthusiasm you need to propel your message deep into the minds of your listeners.

You are qualified to speak on a subject—or "earn the right" as Dale Carnegie put it—when you know more about it than most people, and certainly more than your audience. For example, as R&D manager, you may have researched microchip technology for the past six years. You've earned the right to talk about advances in chip-making. Or you may have completed three different reengineering projects successfully. You've earned the right to train others in your methods. Or, as someone who's run six marathons, you've earned the right to talk about how best to train for one.

Your experiences give you more than knowledge. They've made you enthusiastic about your work. That enthusiasm not only instills in you an urge to talk about your experiences; it also creates an air of excitement that surrounds your talk. The audience sits up and listens.

If that excitement is absent, you put people to sleep.

Sometimes it's not necessary to be have invested a good part of your life in a subject to earn the right to discuss it. Say you're a human resources manager, and your department has been asked to spread the word about a new benefits plan. It probably won't take long to become an expert in the subject. You can qualify yourself to speak with only a few hours' work. Just make sure you do the research necessary.

If you don't feel you are the right person to speak on a subject, decline the invitation. But be honest with yourself; don't let fear deter you. As you'll see, you can control nervousness and even use it to your advantage.

### *Answer Fundamental Questions*

If you are the right person to give the talk, start preparing for it by asking:

- *When is the presentation?* Are you available? Is it at a time of day in which you (and the audience) will be alert?
- *Where will it take place?* Can you get there? Is it a small room or a large hall?
- *What kind of event is it?* Is it a brief overview for a group of your intimates, a keynote address, or something in between? Is it a call to action? Will you speak after a meal or after people have had a few drinks?
- *Who will attend?* Must they attend or is attendance voluntary? What do these people already know about the subject? Are they experts? Neophytes?
- *Why do the organizers want you?* Because you are an acknowledged expert? Because you are the only one available? Because they need to fill up time or because your talk is absolutely critical to a particular effort?
- *How many people will attend?* Ten? A thousand? Whatever the number, know it early so you can prepare yourself.

You can probably think of other questions. The point is to gather as much information as you possibly can about the event and your role in it.

What you discover is, in total, the context for your talk. Knowing the context will help you make many decisions about what information to include, how to present it, how long to talk, and so on. It'll help you *sell* your message to whomever you're speaking to. (And make no mistake—selling a point of view is your job when you give a talk.)

### Make Sure You're Speaking on the Correct Topic

Once you've gathered all the information you need, identify the message or theme—what you want to convey—for your presentation. Check the message out with the person who invited you to speak; make sure it is what he or she had in mind.

You don't want to prepare a talk that isn't of interest to the listeners. It wastes everyone's time and can be mighty embarrassing. (Just ask the woman who spoke for forty-five minutes on creating Easter decorations to a group of Jewish women.)

"Given the audience and the nature of the event," you might say, "I'm assuming these people know what reengineering is and why it's important. I'll title the talk something like, 'Ten Steps to a Successful Reengineering Project.' How does this sound to you?"

This gives the organizer a chance to assess your intent. "That's fine," she may say. But she may respond, "I don't think they know why a reengineering project is valuable. You may have to convince them of that first."

Once you know the context for your talk and have the right theme, it's time to organize your thoughts.

---

## The Agile Manager's Checklist

✔ The first thing to ask yourself: Am I qualified to speak on this subject?

✔ Fundamental questions to ask about any talk you're going to give: who, what, where, how, when, and why?

✔ Be sure your topic is appropriate for the audience.

*Chapter Two*

# Organize Your Thoughts

*The Agile Manager, feet propped on his desk, stared at a small crack in the ceiling without blinking. I have to inform and persuade at the same time, he thought. But I can't persuade explicitly. Tough job.*

*He abruptly swung his feet onto the floor, and pulled in close to the desk. "Yes," he said aloud. Steve, his assistant, heard him through the door and smiled. It was a signal he'd come to know. The Agile Manager would now work blazingly fast until he had his approach down on paper.*

*The bottom line for this talk is simple, he thought. We need to introduce this product line or watch Murphy Technology get to the niche first. And with the cash they acquire from owning that market, they'll have a war chest to make trouble for us in a hundred different ways. But for the board, I'll simply say this product line is crucial for the continued good health of the company. Now, to support that idea . . .*

This chapter covers creating a skeleton, or outline, for your presentation. The next covers putting flesh on that skeleton. Read both before you begin to prepare for a speaking engagement.

### Why Give a Speech or Presentation?

There are really only a few reasons you give business presentations or speeches. The following categories are a starting point for thinking about how to organize your talk.

You speak:

**1. To move people to action.** You want people to do something. For example, you want a potential customer to buy what you're selling. You want your co-workers to do their work in a different fashion. You need your subordinates to change course and follow you into new territory.

In the talk to move people, you ask for action and show your listeners how that action will benefit them. "If we buy this machine, we'll save two hours a week in fabrication time per unit."

To persuade people, said Aristotle a couple thousand years ago, you need to keep three things in mind:

- *Credibility.* People must have reason to believe in you.
- *Emotion.* You must stir the listener's emotions.
- *Logic.* You must use logic to make your case.

To persuade people, use a combination of credibility, logic, and emotion.

**2. To inform.** You know something that other people need or want to know, like how to perform an audit, how to bake the perfect muffin, how to run a machine, or how an exercise program extends your life.

In a talk to inform, you often want to take a listener from the known to the unknown. You can do that by organizing the talk chronologically or by explaining a sequence: "Let me briefly go over the way we now reconcile accounts payable. Then I will explain the new method, which eliminates or consolidates certain steps while adding a new one."

In the talk to inform, limit the scope of your discussion. It's difficult to compress a complex subject into a thirty-minute talk.

Don't even try. Take an important, manageable slice of your subject and discuss it in detail.

**3. To convince.** In the talk to convince, you want to change people's minds. For example, you're an activist and want people to understand the danger greenhouse gasses represent. Or you've seen new equipment in action in Europe and feel your superiors should know about the advantages such equipment brings. Or

**Best Tip**

You'll win over an audience with enthusiasm faster than you will with logic.

your company is pouring resources into a dying business when a golden opportunity lies ready to exploit.

In a talk to convince, first find areas where you all agree. You want people to start thinking "yes" early in the talk: "We all want a healthy planet and clean air to breathe, right?" Or, "We want to keep up with the Europeans, don't we?"

Then show respect for the listeners' point of view. "I understand that some of the provisions of the Clean Air Act cost you money and create aggravation. I own a business myself and know how upset I get when the government ties me up in red tape."

Then demonstrate why it's necessary to change one's point of view. "The bad news is that we're in a dire situation with greenhouse gasses. I'll tell you why. Then I'll tell you how a few modifications to your plant's infrastructure can not only clean up the effluents it produces but save you in cleanup and maintenance costs at the same time."

A key ingredient in a talk to convince: enthusiasm.

Practically, these categories of presentations overlap. The activist wants to convince people but also wants them to change their behavior. The human resources manager mentioned in the last chapter has to explain a new benefits plan. But he also wants people to understand that the new plan is better for them, or better for the company, in the long run. He wants buy-in. While informing, he's persuading. And anyone who tries to get action must also inform.

### Theme: Put the Bottom Line on Top

The best way to begin working on a speech or presentation is at the end. Start with the bottom line, the point of your talk:

- "Getting into the Asian market will increase our sales by 20 percent."
- "If we don't act now, the opportunity I'm about to describe will be lost forever."
- "This product is nothing less than the future of the firm."
- "This new procedure will take three steps out of the manufacturing process and save 15 percent in costs."
- "The service end of the business is more profitable than manufacturing and accounts for half of all sales. We need to put more resources into marketing our services. If we do, sales and profitability will rise."

Starting at the end is, not coincidentally, also the best way to begin your actual presentation. Starting with the conclusion and then providing facts and arguments that support your case is the best way yet invented to grab an audience and keep it interested.

You should be able to state the bottom line, the theme of your talk, in one sentence, or two at the most. If you can't boil your message down to one major idea, then you're probably trying to do too much or cover too many topics.

Explicit in your bottom line should be a benefit for the listener. In a business setting, this could be increased sales, greater profitability, time or money saved, faster inventory turns, higher productivity, expanded capabilities, or more efficient use of resources. The more you tie your message to benefits your listeners will feel and appreciate directly, the more successful your talk will be. Put yourself in the listener's place and ask, "Why should I care about this?"

Thus, a talk about reengineering to senior executives might focus on the financial rewards of handling a process differently. But to those actually doing the work, you'd emphasize an easier workflow, and perhaps the ability to make more decisions independently of meddling managers.

When formulating the bottom line, take a stand. If you believe something—that the company is in trouble, that a procedure could be done a more efficient way, or that the firm must enter a certain market—say so forcefully. If appropriate, ask your listeners to do something. ("Please pull out your checkbooks right now and make a donation. Be as generous as you can. Make it hurt—you'll be doing the world a lot of good.") Or ask them to adopt your point of view.

Start with the point of your presentation—the "bottom line." You'll keep the audience's attention better.

Don't, however, present your case with arrogance, or with a tone that says, "You are ignorant and I'm here to educate you." That turns people against you no matter what you have to say.

Instead, plan to make your case with facts, logic, and personal testimony.

### *Three Ways to Organize the Speech*

Once you have a bottom line in mind, you will often find it easy to come up with an organizational scheme for presenting it.

Aristotle pointed out that a good speech needs only two things: exposition (in which you provide facts and introduce ideas) and proof (in which you offer convincing arguments and evidence). That leaves lots of room to tailor your presentation to the audience.

Here are three good ways to organize a presentation, and include exposition and proof, in your talk:

**1. AIDA.** This method is one advocated by many speaking

(and writing) professionals. The acronym stands for:

- Win their **A**ttention
- Arouse their **I**nterest
- Create a **D**esire
- Stimulate **A**ction or **A**greement

You win attention with a good opening (discussed in the next chapter). You arouse interest by offering moving testimony that shows why listeners should care about your topic. You create a desire by offering facts and evidence that convinces. And you stimulate action or agreement by asking for action and showing listeners why it's in their interest to do so.

No matter how you organize a speech, plan to win the audience's attention at the beginning.

**2. Chronological.** Time underlies this organizing method, useful in the talks to persuade or inform. The speech has three parts:

- "Where we've been." Call up an antiquated or quaint past.
- "Where we are today." Show how far you and your audience have come since then.
- "Where we need to be tomorrow." Explain where you and the audience need to head to be successful in coming years.

**3. The 3 X 3 method.** This is an excellent way to organize a speech to convince or persuade. Start with your theme, and come up with three main points to support it. Under each main point, offer three supporting reasons. The first main point should be the strongest, and the last should lead into your conclusion, which restates your theme and the benefits for your listeners.

Imagine, for instance, that you are trying to convince the directors of the company you work for, a printer, to buy a new printing press.

**Theme:** "Buying a press with expanded capabilities will provide many benefits, including increased sales and profitability."

**Point one: We need the press to keep up with demand.**
—It will eliminate our perennial problem with backlogs
—It will mean we won't have to turn away work
—It will increase our versatility
**Point two: We can use it to sell into new markets.**
—We'll be able to do more four-color work, which means we can start printing magazines
—We'll do shorter runs more economically, letting us compete with quick-print shops
—We can market outside of the tri-state area
**Point three: It will create efficiencies that fall to the bottom line.**
—Speeding up the operation will result in reduced labor costs per job and faster turnover of paper inventory
—With the addition of the new machine, return on assets will rise to at least 8 percent
—The payback period for the press is only three years
**Conclusion:** If we buy a new printing press, we'll increase sales and profitability.

If you're having trouble coming up with a "bottom line" or an outline, let your subconscious mind do the hard work. Tell yourself just before you fall asleep that you need a theme and organizational scheme. Part of your brain will set to work on the problem and will often present a solution the very next morning.

Finally, whatever organizing method you use, be sure not to cover too much ground or make too many points. Speaking is different than writing. Your listeners can't rewind your talk to think about a certain point more deeply, and they can't stop you at will to reflect on your words. It pays to be simple, clear, and focused on presenting one message and one message only.

### Don't Read a Speech or Presentation

Before we continue, a word of caution: Don't plan to write out your presentation and read it in front of a group. While you may feel that reading a speech is the only way to remember all the important points—or maintain control of your fear—it usually bores an audience. You'll lose people in the first few minutes and never get them back.

To release all your energy and enthusiasm for a subject, you must interact with people. You can't do that by gripping a lectern tightly and staring at a piece of paper. Also, writing out and reading a speech tends to make it more formal, which creates a barrier between you and the audience.

Note: Some people like to write out a speech first, even if they have no intention of reading it, to capture a stream of thoughts. Write out the speech if it helps. But be sure to boil it down to a more useful form by creating notes or an outline from it.

Public speaking expert Terry Pearce recommends writing out a speech to better spot unclear or fuzzy thinking. Do so if you think it's necessary, but practicing the speech, or parts of it, in front of your spouse or a friend can provide similar feedback.

### Create Notes or an Outline

With a clear bottom line and organizational scheme in mind, you can begin to draft notes or an outline for your speech. Either notes or an outline should include your bottom line contained in a strong opening, supporting reasons or arguments, and a conclusion that summarizes your main points and restates the bottom line.

Plan to get out in front of the podium or lectern. You'll engage people better and come across as "just folks."

Before you take these initial notes up to the podium with you, boil them down to a bare outline or a series of cards that contain key words. If you rehearse enough, that outline or set of note cards will serve to jog your memory. If you use notes any more extensive than that, you'll end up reading to the audience.

Some things to keep in mind as you draft notes:

- Keep a small notebook with you. As you go about your daily business, part of your mind will be working on your speech. You may have spontaneous thoughts about what to include, what facts support your case, and so forth. These jottings will come in handy as you work on your notes.

**Best Tip**

Anticipate objections to your message. Address doubts your listeners will have before you get to the Q&A session.

- Remember to talk, in all parts of the speech, in terms of benefits and the audience's interests. Never lose sight of "What's in it for them?"

- Keep it simple—simple points, simple arguments, simple facts.

- If you do no more than state a strong bottom line, offer three strong supporting arguments, and conclude with power, you've done a lot.

- Appeal to higher values and noble virtues. Whether or not people act accordingly to the Golden Rule, they like to believe they do. Don't be afraid to build a speech around concepts like honor, loyalty, teamwork, sharing, and so forth. In a sense, you show an audience respect when you assume they operate on a higher plane than their fellow humans. They'll respect you more in return.

- Anticipate objections. If you're facing a hostile audience, or merely an inquisitive one, disarm it by answering the questions—especially the tough ones—you know it will have.

- Your presentation should flow logically, with one point leading naturally into the next. Pay careful attention to transitions—how you're going to exit one argument and begin another. Further, make sure the audience gets the point. Say things like, "What I'm about to say is at the heart of this presentation," or "This next idea is really important."

- Bear in mind that it's a rare person who will stay tuned in to you for the entire length of the presentation. Even those that do will forget 30 to 50 percent of what you've said after half an hour. Don't be afraid to repeat yourself. If your talk is longer than ten or fifteen minutes, summarize key points occasionally. You can also stop every so often to take questions or otherwise make sure that everyone is with you.

## The Agile Manager's Checklist

✔ Decide whether you want to move people to action, inform, or convince.

✔ Always start out with the "bottom line"—the point or conclusion of your talk.

✔ Whatever the topic, take a stand.

✔ Never read a speech or presentation.

✔ Always talk in terms of benefits. Never lose sight of the listener who's thinking, "What's in it for me?"

*Chapter Three*

# Flesh Out Your Presentation

The Agile Manager sat at his desk in a rare night session at work. He rolled two marbles around on the top of his desk while searching his mind for the perfect opening. If he didn't grab his audience at the beginning, he knew, all else was for naught.

He picked up a marble and bounced it twice. The suspense opening, he thought. That might work. Let's see if I can get it right. He pushed the marbles into a desk drawer.

He began to write, "There's a market that I hadn't imagined existed until I and some of the others in our group heard about it at a conference a year and a half ago. You probably aren't aware of it at all. Some people think it doesn't exist and never will, while others think it will have worldwide sales in excess of $10 billion just five years from now.

"We are convinced this market does exist. We also think we can create a product line to serve it based on the work we've done for the company's current market-leading line in medical instrumentation. That line offers all the technology and manufacturing know-how we need to get in on the ground floor of this emerging market.

"Getting in on the ground floor and riding the elevator up, we believe, will result in sales of $4 million next year, twice that the *following year, and ten times that—$40 million—in year three. And those revenue streams will be growing while those for the main product line flatten out and begin to decline.*

*"That's why I think pursuing this market is absolutely essential for the long-term health of the company.*

*"What is this mystery market? Most people call it . . ."*

*The Agile Manager smiled. He'd have to tighten up that opening and get to the point quicker, he knew, but it ought to grab them.*

Preparing the presentation is not difficult once you've got a strong theme and a basic organizational outline in mind. You have to create an opening and conclusion, fill in the body with proof, add an emotional angle by telling personal stories, and make sure it all flows in a smooth, logical manner.

It is in these details, however, that many a talk fails.

### Speak Conversationally

Here's probably the best advice contained in this book: When you speak to an audience, speak to it as though you were conversing with a friend or to a small group of people by the water cooler. That advice goes whether you're speaking to 5 people in a small conference room or 450 in a large hall.

There's no value in using big words you wouldn't use in normal conversation, for example, or in constructing a lofty speech based on classical principles of speechmaking. These get in the way of making a point.

Your job is to communicate an important message. You can do that best by being yourself and speaking (and gesturing) the way you would to a good friend using clear, simple language.

### Devise an Attention-Grabbing Title and Opening

If possible, state the bottom line in the title of the presentation: "How New Order Fulfillment Software Saved Us $1.5 million" or "Live Longer, Feel Better with Exercise."

If you're clever, you can create suspense with a title. I once heard an excellent entertaining talk called, "Take my Grandmother, Please!" The title alone intrigued people and made us more attentive as the speaker began. (The talk was on popular myths, and the title referred to one of the most prominent: A friend of a friend of a friend's grandmother died in Mexico on a vacation and he couldn't get the body out of the country—or buried in it.)

**Best Tip**

Can't find a good quote to open a speech? Start with a personal story. You'll connect with the audience faster.

The opening, however, is more important than the title. If you hook your listeners from the start, you're on your way to making a big impression or getting action from them.

There are many useful ways to begin a speech or presentation. Start with a:

- Quote
- Personal experience or anecdote
- Startling fact
- Question
- Historical story
- Humorous story
- Recent event or incident
- Suspenseful story
- Prediction
- Promise to improve the listener's life

Whichever form you choose, the opening should lead naturally into your bottom line. ("That story, as you can all see, underscores the importance of following safety procedures. As I'll show in this talk, following the company's safety guidelines will improve your chances of avoiding an accident here by 30 percent.")

**Establish Credibility.** Another important concern in the opening is to establish your credibility. If you're lucky enough to have had a competent introduction, that may have been taken care of. ("Dr. Smith is the author of sixteen articles and two books on recombinant DNA. When people talk of the giants in this field, his name invariably comes up.") But don't count on the moderator or master of ceremonies to do a competent job introducing you; they rarely do.

**Best Tip**

If the person introducing you fails to establish your credibility, do it yourself.

There are a hundred ways to establish credibility. One is simply to state facts. "Who am I to speak on this subject? I've overseen the breeding of more than a thousand thoroughbreds. Six of these horses have won major events, including two Kentucky Derbies. Another 253 have won regional events."

You can also use a personal anecdote to both open strongly and establish credibility: "You know, a funny thing happened to me in the lab last year. I was playing around with a compound that suddenly disappeared before my eyes. 'Why did that happen?' I wondered. Well, answering that question took me six months, but it led to the largest grant ever awarded by the National Science Foundation. Here's why I got that money . . ."

A prop can establish credibility. I gave a talk not long ago on the benefits of exercise. To open, I held up a running shoe and said, "This shoe, according to my logbook, has covered 563 miles on the roads since March 1. Why am I showing it to you? Because it symbolizes my commitment to keeping fit and all the benefits that regular exercise provides . . ."

**Create a Road Map for the Audience.** Sometimes it's appropriate to use the opening to explain where you will be going with the talk. This is especially helpful if the presentation is unavoidably lengthy or complicated: "In this presentation, I'm going to show you exactly how I saved Orange Airlines $62 million over two years. First I'll discuss the steps involved in rerouting all the airplanes, then I'll talk about how we implemented the new schedule, then I'll discuss the overall financial results and what Orange did with the savings."

People like to know where they are headed and why. Outlining a talk for an audience gives it a mental road map it can follow as you speak.

**Resist Banalities.** Banish banalities from your opening. These include, "It's a pleasure to be here," or "I'm honored to have been asked to speak tonight." Everybody says these things; few in the audience believe them. ("I'm delighted to be here," she said as her face became ashen and sweat trickled down her brow.)

If it's really an honor, go ahead and say so—but explain why: "I've long admired the work of the society, and Ken Jones and Mary Mattera are two of the most brilliant consultants I've ever worked with. For them to ask me to speak is most flattering."

**Practice the Opening.** Though in general you don't want to memorize a speech, sometimes it helps put your nerves at ease if you practice your opening many times. If you start off strongly, your confidence soars.

Fix the opening in your mind and resist the urge to tinker with it or change it at the last moment.

### *Fill the Body of the Presentation*

After a strong opening, fill in the details: offer proof that supports your bottom line, give moving personal testimony, draw apt analogies, and more. These are all what one astute speaker and writer, Deborah Flores, calls "mental fasteners"—because they help fix your message in the mind of the listener.

**Best Tip**

Practice your opening over and over.

Not using such fasteners is a common mistake, especially among the academic crowd. Many people speak in generalizations and abstractions. Even if these are presented in a lively manner, the message doesn't stick. It takes colorful, concrete language to do that.

Here's a look at some effective fasteners:

**Personal anecdotes.** Nothing builds ties to an audience faster or better than a good personal story. And personal "proof" is as powerful as it comes. Imagine you are discussing plant safety to a group of shop-floor workers. You say,

> I'll never forget the time I witnessed an accident that could have resulted in several deaths. A man was driving a forklift around the warehouse on 26th Street. There were some painters on a scaffold two stories high painting window frames.
>
> Well, the guy on the forklift wasn't watching where he was going, and he plowed right into the scaffolding. One end started to buckle, shaking the platform hard. One of the painters slipped and was hanging by one arm from a crossbar. I saw the whole thing unfolding before my eyes, and I started running. I feared the worst. But when I got there . . .

I once heard a speech in which a woman explained what it was like being anesthetized just before surgery. She talked about the cold feel of the steel hospital cart, the murmuring voices in the corridor, the anesthesiologist's breathing rate, the mysterious feeling that some benevolent spirit was lying next to her, and the sinking feeling as she passed out.

Stories like these have people on the edge of their seats. And they offer a real advantage: Because you were there, it becomes easy for you to become animated as you relive the experience. Your movements and gestures will be spontaneous and believable. That doubles the impact of the story.

**Statistics.** Though often misused, statistics stay with people. "Look around the room. Two out of every five men here, 40 percent, are going to have some symptoms of heart disease by the age of sixty-five." Or, "Venture capitalists lose money in most of their ventures. In fact, they expect only 10 percent of their projects to make money. But that sickly batting average of .100 is enough for some of them to become rich as Croesus." Or, "Our return on sales has averaged 8.9 percent over the past ten years."

**Facts.** You can't beat facts. If company A adopted your technology and saved $10,000 a month, by all means say so. If two recent scientific discoveries promise a breakthrough in radiation therapy, don't withhold that information. If country X won a war based on a particular strategy, tell it like it is. In general, the testimony of experts on a subject carries a lot of weight—especially if you're the expert.

If you use statistics, relate them to the audience—"That's 3.4 television sets for each one of you in this room."

**Quotations.** Nothing beats a good quote, right? " 'All history is a record of the power of minorities, and of minorities of one,' said Ralph Waldo Emerson. That's as true now as it was when Emerson wrote it in the nineteenth century. Look at Serbian leader Slobodan Milosevic . . ."

Yes, quotations are the workhorses of many a speech. And that's a problem. For one thing, you hear the same people quoted again and again: Churchill, Lincoln, Emerson, Roosevelt, Kennedy. I've even heard speakers use the same quote on the same day at a conference.

Also, because people tend to repeat quotes they hear, quotes are often misstated. For instance, business bashers love to repeat in derisive tones what they believe Charles Wilson, head of General Motors, said back in 1953: "What's good for General Motors is good for the United States." The trouble is, that's not what he said. He actually said, "What's good for the country is good for General Motors and vice versa." Not quite the arrogant statement you're often led to believe, is it?

Speech expert Terry Pearce, in the book *Leading Out Loud*, says speakers should always be authentic. For him that means whenever you tell a story or offer a quote, it should have personal relevance to you. It shouldn't be something you just pulled out of *The Columbia Dictionary of Quotations*. If you're going to quote John F. Kennedy, for example, read the entire speech, or a good part of it, so you know the context for the quote. And don't quote Shakespeare gratuitously; quote him if the line is part of a sonnet you memorized in high school and have always remembered, or if it captures exactly how you felt when you were first in love at age eighteen. Pearce makes a good point, for authenticity is at the heart of your credibility.

---

**Best Tip**

Tell stories or offer quotes only if they have personal meaning for you, not because other speakers use them.

---

**Historical stories.** History provides many apt examples of the points you are making. And when you use stories that include well-known people, it can add credibility. For example, say you are discussing the need to introduce a just-in-time inventory program with an audience that is skeptical of "foreign" ideas. It helps to be able to say,

> You may think that Japanese work processes can't work here. Just-in-time is a practice, you may believe, too closely based on the Japanese culture. Well, I've got news for you. Henry Ford was running a just-in-time system back in the 1920s. 'I am proud to say,' Ford wrote in 1926, 'That our company doesn't own or use a single warehouse.' Ford's Fordson plant, in fact, had five railroad tracks running into it, which dropped off the raw materials needed that day. Just in time? You bet.

Be careful that you don't use the many stories that have by now become clichéd and overused. For example, who by now hasn't heard the story of the 3M employee who, faced with a problem of finding hymns quickly at choir practice, invented Post-it notes? Or the story of how Fred Smith received a C– for his business-school business plan for Federal Express?

You can add power to your speeches and stand out from the crowd by finding original stories based on your own research. Again, go with the authentic.

**Analogies.** A good analogy goes a long way toward simplifying a topic and keeping it foremost in people's minds. In a recent book based on speeches called *The Future of Capitalism*, Lester Thurow likened the world economy to a set of tectonic plates that move underground and produce large and small changes at the surface, including earthquakes. He carried the analogy throughout the book most effectively.

It takes mental effort to come up with a good analogy that works for you and to which the audience can relate. But it's not all that hard to see how your subject is like another. To get your mind working, here are a few sample analogies:

- Product development: The process of conceiving, carrying, and delivering a baby.
- A partnership or alliance with another firm: A marriage.
- Building a business: Preparing for, training, and running a marathon.
- Downsizing/restructuring: A fat person undergoing a regimen of dieting, habit changing, and exercise.
- Building a new facility: A family adds on to the house with the arrival of new members or as its interests change.
- How a computer works: How a human brain works.

Analogies put the unknown in familiar terms, and thus help your ideas create an impact in the mind of the listener.

**Colorful language.** Effective speakers create vivid mental pictures in people's minds. If you speak strictly in abstract terms or generalizations, you're not creating pictures. For example, a dry speaker might say, "The sea was rough that day." A speaker who wanted to tug harder on the audience's emotions would say, "The sea was a funny color—the peaks of the gray swells looked like whipped cream. I sat in the stern of the boat, which would rise eight or ten feet, then come down with a crash as the wave passed underneath us." As you

**Best Tip**

Pick words designed to stick in your listeners' minds. The best refer to concrete objects or ideas in the real world.

told this story, you could use hand gestures to show how the sea rose and fell, and clap your hand when the boat hit the sea with a crash.

Here's a short list of other ways to create vivid imagery using comparisons:

- *Use metaphors.* A metaphor compares two different things directly: "That man is a shark," or "My office is a garbage dump."
- *Use similes.* A simile also compares different things, but uses "like" or "as" to do it: "Be careful of him—he's like Rasputin." "She's as happy as someone who just won the Lotto jackpot."
- *Contrast the strange with the familiar.* One speaker I heard, for example, compared a house on a bright sunny morning with the same house at midnight on Halloween. The contrast sent shivers up my spine.
- *Compare the worst and best cases.* "If we do nothing now, next year at this time you'll see five hundred workers handed pink slips—probably around Christmas. But if we take the action I've proposed, those same factory hands will not only keep their jobs, they'll be working overtime to keep up with demand. Rather than handing them a pink slip, we'll be in a position to hand them a turkey—and a nice bonus check."

**Visual aids.** Visual aids are so useful to a speaker that all of chapter seven is devoted to the subject.

**Humor.** A good joke or humorous story holds the interest of the audience, and it creates a hook to hang an idea upon.

If you can tell a good joke or story, do it. Just make sure it's in good taste. If in doubt, try the joke or story out on someone first.

If you're the kind of person that can't remember jokes well, be careful. By no means learn jokes because you feel you must; it's never absolutely necessary.

But each of you makes people laugh occasionally. Take note—either in your mind or on paper—when you do. It's possible you've created material that could make a group laugh, even if you're not a humorist in the traditional sense.

Comedy writer and speaker Gene Perret, writing in the August 1996 issue of *The Toastmaster*, recommends you mine sources regularly for humorous material. Write down jokes you see in magazines or newspapers, as well as those you hear on TV,

**Best Tip**

Write down jokes you hear or read, but only if they tickle your funny bone.

the radio, or in conversation with friends. This method, he says, allows anyone to start "assembling a repertoire of humor."

A joke or humorous story should amplify or augment a point you're making. Never tell a joke that has nothing to do with your talk; these often fall flat and embarrass you.

**Simplify and personalize facts.** How often have you heard a speaker say something like, "That's the largest forest in the world." Or, worse, "The forest covers fifteen million hectares."

It's not hard to make dry facts like these more vivid in the minds of listeners. I once heard a speaker talk of the vastness of Siberia. How vast is it? You could take the entire continental United States, he said, and drop it inside Siberia and have room to spare on all sides.

He went on to discuss its forest resources. But rather than quote quantities, he simply said that Siberia has more timber than all that in the entire United States, and that it had a full quarter of the world's known timber reserves.

When you simplify and personalize facts, you not only put them in terms people can understand. You also create an image that can stick in the mind for years.

Another way to personalize facts is to relate them to the audience directly. When speaking of the overall consumption of beer, for example, you make it personal by saying something like, "that's nine gallons of beer a year for everyone in this room. And when you take out the 25 percent of the population that rarely drinks, we're talking twelve gallons a person. And twelve gallons is 5.3 cases." People don't understand 973,000,000 gallons. But they understand five cases of beer out in the garage.

**Best Tip**

Give it all you've got until you hear the applause. Then you can relax.

**Use threes.** I don't know why, but people respond to items grouped in threes. Maybe it's because threes appear so often in our lives—Father, Son, and the Holy Ghost; vini, vidi, vici; stop, drop, and roll; the legislative branch, the judicial branch, and the executive branch; and so on.

You can use threes to organize your speech, as mentioned: three main points, with three more points to support each. But also use threes for rhetorical flourishes: "If we act now, we can expect higher sales, lower costs, and bigger profits." "What can save us from the superficial commercialism of Christmas? It's simple—faith, hope, and charity."

**Use dialogue.** Demosthenes, the most famous of the ancient Greek orators, liked to use rhetorical dialogues between himself and imagined opponents. You can do the same with great effect. For example,

> I imagine some of you are thinking, "Come on Joe, give me a break. Of course anybody who lifts weights for two hours a day can add three inches to their biceps in six months. But who has two hours a day?" Well, I'm here to tell you that you don't need two hours a day. All you need is twenty minutes. . . .

### Stay Strong Through the Finish

Like a runner racing ten thousand meters, you must finish strong through the tape.

You've already given the bottom line, and you've supported your argument with facts, personal anecdotes, a good joke or story, and more. Now it's time to summarize your talk and re-state the bottom line, either explicitly or in another way, and remind people of the benefit for them if they do what you ask.

> It's time for me to finish up. You know by now how I feel—that the ad campaign we've created for you will result in a market share increase of four points. Most advertising people wouldn't go out on a limb like that, but I know we can get that increase for you because of the innovative appeals we'll make for your brand. These are based, remember, first on the university study that showed how the use of color influences buyers. We'll get that four-point increase by also using the Internet—and I showed you how cost-effective that can be. And we'll get you that four-point increase by making a strong showing at trade shows and conferences, an area you've neglected.
>
> Choose us to do your campaign. If you do, that four-point in-crease in market share will increase your sales by $420,000 a year. Thanks for giving me your time.

## The Agile Manager's Checklist

✔ Always speak in a conversational tone, and use common words. Pretend you're talking to a few friends around the lunch table.

✔ Keep trying until you come up with an interesting open-ing.

✔ Let your listeners know where you're headed in the talk.

✔ If you can tell a good (inoffensive) joke, do it. But don't feel you must.

✔ At the end, summarize your main points and restate the conclusion.

*Chapter Four*

# Rehearse!

The Agile Manager had propped the outline up on the window sill above his desk. As he paced back and forth practicing his presentation, he glanced at it now and then to remind himself of the next point. He never used notes; he preferred an outline with three main points between the opening and conclusion. These three points were:

—The Future of the Company
—New Markets
—Financial Results

Under each point were three to five key phrases like "market share," "sales figures," and "development costs." Each main point and key phrase would trigger in his mind the appropriate fact, story, or argument.

Because all the other offices were empty except Marty's down the hall, the Agile Manager practiced at full volume with no self-consciousness. (Marty, the quality manager and a workaholic, liked seeing the Agile Manager at work two evenings in a row. Maybe someone had spoken to him about his slacker tendencies, he thought with glee.)

After the fourth try, the words seemed to come naturally for each *point he wanted to make. Not that they came out exactly the same each time; they didn't. But he'd created what he liked to think of as a groove, and as long as he stayed in it he'd be understandable at the least and eloquent at best.*

*He started to relax.*

Some people organize their presentation, come up with a few facts, apt analogies, and anecdotes, and then wing it when it comes time to present. After all, they think beforehand, I know what I want to say, and I've got the notes. How hard can it be?

Very hard. "Winging" a presentation is a mistake no one makes twice. Every experienced presenter knows how important it is to rehearse a presentation or speech.

**Best Tip**

Practice your presentation. "Winging" a talk is a mistake nobody makes twice.

If you don't rehearse, you'll rely on your notes too much and end up reading the speech.

If you don't rehearse, you can't imagine how facing an audience will change your ability to deliver a presentation. Giving a speech isn't a one-way affair. It's interactive even when the audience remains silent. People communicate with you in ways other than words.

If you don't rehearse, you won't know how long your speech is. And if you fill a thirty-minute spot with a twenty-minute speech, the organizers will be mad. If you take forty-five minutes, your audience will be mad, too.

If you don't rehearse, you won't know that one of your points is too complex, or that your transitions are awkward.

### How to Rehearse

Your goal is to deliver the presentation or speech looking straight at your audience 96 percent of the time (perhaps a little bit less if you're writing on a flip chart). The other 4 percent is for glancing at notes or an outline. If you're looking at your notes more than that, it will distract the audience and you'll most likely fumble with the words.

By practicing, you fix in your mind the point you want to get across. How you say it will vary from practice session to practice session, but after a while the words will come out about the same each time.

**Best Tip**

Practice your presentation in front of your spouse or a friend. Ask for candid feedback.

Use your outline or notes, then, to jog your memory as to what comes next.

Glance at your notes, find the point, make it. Glance down again briefly to find the next point, and make it. And so on.

If you practice enough, you'll find that you can often make a number of points in a row without looking at the outline. One will naturally lead into the next.

If you find yourself saying the speech or presentation almost exactly the same way each time, be careful. It's possible you're over-practicing. Leave a little to chance in a presentation; it adds spice and zest to your talk. And it gives you room to improvise—and that's when some of your best lines will come out.

### Ways to Rehearse

Take advantage of all these methods to rehearse:

**Rehearse alone:** The most obvious way to rehearse is to take your notes or outline, head to a deserted room, and do your presentation as many times as you must to feel comfortable.

An advantage of practicing in a place away from others: You'll be uninhibited and can try out different things.

**Rehearse for friends or family.** Do your presentation at least once in front of someone else you trust to point out the good aspects and those that could be improved. If it's long, you can stop periodically for quick evaluations, and you can do spots over again.

If you're concerned about some aspect of the talk, like whether the opening is strong enough or whether you're offering enough proof, tell your spouse or friend beforehand to see if your fear is well-founded.

**Rehearse in front of a video camera or tape recorder.** Tapes don't lie. Use them to evaluate yourself. Audiotape recorders can be especially beneficial for evaluating the speed of your delivery, the rate at which you vary your pitch and emphasis, and the logical framework of your talk. Listening without seeing yourself helps you focus on the words.

In particular, look for places you could simplify or cut your speech. It's a rare speech that couldn't stand either. Also, watch for awkward transitions, weak openings and conclusions, and places where a good "fastener" would add power.

**Rehearse informally.** Say you want to include a humorous story or personal anecdote in a speech and don't know how it will come off. Tell the story to a friend over lunch or out on the golf course to get a reaction. Don't tell the other person your ulterior purpose; just gauge his or her reaction. "Harry, a funny thing happened to me when I was in Bermuda last month. I walked into my hotel room and found another guest going through my suitcase. I was about to slug him when . . ."

You can also test your opinions this way: "You know Doris, I've been thinking about the utilization rates of our sewing machines, and I wonder whether we should scrap the lot of them and buy one of those new machines put out by Soclo Industries. What do you think?"

**Best Tip**

Join Toastmasters. If you don't know where the nearest club is, call 1–714–858–8255 or visit *www.toastmasters.org*.

**Rehearse at Toastmasters.** I've seen people give keynote

addresses, conference presentations, fund-raising speeches, testi-
monials, introductions, and sales presentations at the Toastmasters chapter I belong to. It can be enormously helpful to "pre-
view" such speeches and presentations to a group of friendly, yet
rigorous, evaluators. Doing so invariably sharpens and adds power
to a speech.

### Practice How Often?

How often should you practice? Until you feel comfortable.
For some people, this takes but two or three rehearsals. For others—myself included—it means doing your complete presentation six to eight times, or even more often if it's short.

I also like to spread practice time over a number of days. In
the week preceding the speech or presentation, for example, I'll
do it twice each night, and perhaps put in a little extra work on
the opening or conclusion.

---

### The Agile Manager's Checklist

✔ Rehearse so you don't end up reading your speech.
✔ Rehearse so you know how long your speech is.
✔ Rehearse so you can be looking at your audience 96
percent of the time.
✔ Rehearse by telling stories in your speech informally to
friends.
✔ Rehearse the entire presentation until you feel comfort
able—at least two or three times.

# Increase Your Impact
# On the Audience

*"Enthusiasm is the yeast that makes
your hope rise to the stars."*

HENRY FORD

*Chapter Five*

# Control Your Nerves

The Agile Manager sat in a plush rocker he kept in the corner of his office. The big presentation was still a few days away, but he'd learned a long time ago to practice facing a group in his mind.

With his eyes closed, he imagined striding into the conference room, a big smile on his face, shaking hands with all the directors. "I've heard a lot about you," one said to him. Said another, "I'm looking forward to hearing about the new product line. I understand you consider it extremely important for the health of company."

He performed his opening and noticed every pair of eyes in the room focused on him intently. A couple of the directors nodded as he talked, another smiled. One scowled at times; the Agile Manager made a note to speak to him directly when he addressed objections to the plan.

He then fast-forwarded through the body of the presentation and came to his conclusion. What kind of reaction did he want? Applause? Silence? Murmurs of approval? In this situation, the board would probably be silent until the chairman said a few words to signal his position and ask for questions.

The Agile Manager performed a stunning summation in his mind, using a strong, clear voice throughout, while watching faces in-

*tently. Two of the board members began to smile but bit their lips. The scowler still scowled. But the others all looked as though they were weighing him as well as the strategy he'd just outlined. That was good, he decided.*

*He opened his eyes and looked around the office. Would the presentation turn out just this way? Probably not. Yet he never forgot the time he visualized doing a presentation at Midwest Bank Corp. for a major line of credit and seeing a stubborn banker asking well-pointed questions about collateral. Then, after the actual presentation, a banker on the loan committee asked some of those very same questions.*

*After that, he was a believer in doing dry runs in the mind. There was magic in them he didn't understand, but which he could use.*

*Now, thought the Agile Manager, how am I going to handle that scowling director?*

You'll probably never get over your nervousness before a speech or a presentation. Even the most accomplished speakers feel the butterflies before getting up in front of the audience.

And that's as it should be. Ponder this old saying: If a speaker is as cool as a cucumber, he's probably about as interesting as one.

You can learn to use your nervousness and the adrenaline it produces to fuel your enthusiasm for the subject, to amplify your voice or body language, and to keep you sharp and alert when facing a discriminating audience.

Nervous energy is far different than the terror some people feel at the thought of giving a speech. Terror disables you; nervous energy channeled properly drives up the octane level of your talk.

The key, then, is to turn terror into useful energy. Each of the following sections shows how to do that.

### Be Prepared

Be ready for your presentation. That means making sure you have the right message for the audience, that you've outlined the talk in a logical way, that you've added colorful elements to make the presentation memorable, and that you've rehearsed it well enough that you could do it in your sleep. (No, there's no way to take shortcuts when preparing for a presentation. Shortcuts lead to failure.)

### What Are You Afraid Of?

If you're afraid of giving a presentation, ask yourself exactly what you fear. Forgetting your words? Fumbling the opening or conclusion? Tripping over a microphone cord? Giving weak answers to hostile questions? Speaking with your zipper open?

Pinpoint your fears, then prepare or practice to ensure they don't come true.

Maybe your fear is serving you well—your opening *is* weak, or you haven't thought up good answers to some of the questions you know you'll get. Do whatever is necessary to turn the weakness into strength. Normally this means more practice, but it may mean an additional trip to the library or cyberspace to do more research.

As for irrational fears, like talking with your zipper open, make a note to check it just before you talk.

But you can also ask yourself, so what? Even if I trip, what's the worst that can happen? Will I get fired? No. Will my message lose impact? Probably not. Will I be embarrassed? Perhaps, but I'll survive that.

### Visualize the Outcome

Many a professional speaker makes a key recommendation: Visualize your talk, especially the outcome. Such mental preparation has a strange way of mirroring how things actually turn out.

Sit in a chair in a quiet room, close your eyes, and take a few deep breaths. See yourself standing in front of the group. See people smile and nod at you throughout the talk, see them clap long and hard after you're done, see them come up to you after it's over to congratulate you and ask additional questions, and see your boss praise your effort.

### Inspect the Room

Remember Murphy's Law: If it can happen, it will. Another way to put yourself at ease, therefore, is to check out the room you are to speak in before you give your talk. Your goal: to ensure nothing *can* go wrong. Consider the following:

- *The configuration of the room.* Is the podium placed where you want it? Are the chairs arranged in a way conducive to your talk? Will lights shine in your eyes? Will everyone be able to see your flip chart?

- *The temperature.* People heat up a room quickly, especially small rooms. If it's already warm with no one in it, reduce the temperature. You don't need an additional reason to sweat.

> **Best Tip**
>
> Inspect the room you're going to speak in well before people arrive.

- *Audiovisual equipment.* Does the overhead projector work properly? Is there a spare bulb nearby? Do you know how to replace it at a moment's notice? Is the computer keyboard like the one you use?

- *Cables and wires.* Are wires taped down and out of the way? If there is an awkward bump in the floor due to wires, can you work around it? Is the microphone wire long enough for you to move around? (Some pros loop it once or twice around their belts so they don't accidentally tug the wire out of its socket.)

- *Rooms next door.* Is it possible that a loud function may be going on next door? I once gave a talk in a room next to a loud party. Another time I watched a hapless speaker compete with the clattering dishes of a hotel kitchen on the other side of the wall. (Sometimes you can move to another room. At the very least, you'll be mentally prepared for competition for your attention.)

- *Water.* Make sure you have water within reach.

## Avoid Perfectionism

Psychotherapist and accomplished speaker Judith Pearson counsels people on phobias and managing stress. Her clientele includes people afraid to speak in public, and from them she's identified a disabler to be aware of: perfectionism.

Many people, she writes, are afraid to speak because they fear making mistakes. Yet every speaker, even the most experienced, makes mistakes. "The secret to superb speaking," she wrote in the March 1996 issue of *The Toastmaster*, "is to give yourself permission to make mistakes and learn to recover from them quickly."

If you make a mistake, make amends if necessary, focus on what comes next, and move on. Dwelling on the error can weaken the rest of your speech.

Audiences, she reminds us, are forgiving. She's absolutely right. People want you to succeed. And besides, many won't even notice the mistake that looms large in your mind. I once thought I'd bungled the conclusion of a speech; several people later complimented me on its power.

## Just Before the Presentation

You're seated in the presentation room, listening as the moderator or toastmaster is introducing you to the audience. Your heart starts to race and your palms get sweaty.

This is normal. But it's critical you get your emotions under control. To do that:

**Breathe deeply.** Focus on breathing deeply from the diaphragm. Do ten long, slow breaths just before you go up. The increased oxygen will help calm you.

**Give yourself a pep talk.** "OK, old buddy. It's time. You can do it. You'll floor 'em."

**Recite the first few opening lines in your mind.** They'll pop out of your mouth with vigor when you begin to speak.

**Remind yourself to start slowly.** Your energy may cause you to race through the opening. Rein in your energy so you can use it for the whole presentation.

You don't want to relax completely—if that were possible. You want to use the energy building in your bones for a strong start to the talk.

| Best Tip |
| --- |
| When you begin, look for a few friendly faces in the audience. Speak directly to them. |

One last thing. If you're giving a presentation to people in your own company, be sure to take ten minutes or so to prepare. Don't sit at your desk taking phone calls or answering e-mail. You don't want pre-speech distractions to color your talk.

### As You're Speaking

When you begin to speak, look for some friendly faces in the audience and direct your comments to them. If you fix on someone who looks bored or hostile, you may lose confidence, and you need all of that you can get. (As you move through the talk, you'll gain confidence. A fun game is to speak to the bored to see if you can make them come alive.) Finding friendly faces to speak to reminds you that your talk is really just a conversation with people who care about what you have to say.

Some people recommend that you imagine the entire audience naked or in their underwear. It's a way to remind yourself that you're all just people here to learn something or have a good time. I've never tried this method; I've always been afraid I'd begin to laugh.

Here's another ploy to put yourself on even footing with an audience: Imagine everyone you're speaking to is there to ask you for a favor—lend them money, find them a job, arrange a date with your sister, or whatever.

Once you get rolling, you'll find your eyes gravitating to those who are clearly listening to what you have to say. That's fine; just make sure you're not speaking to one or two people only. Find at least four or five people in different parts of the room to talk to.

Don't forget: In most situations, people in the audience are on your side. They want you to succeed, they want you to tell them things they don't know, they want you to give them reasons to act in a certain way or to believe something. Most of them are not viewing you critically or judging you.

### *The Best Way to Control Nerves*

Speak often in front of people. The more you do, the better you'll get at turning simple fear into a form of invigorating energy that makes you feel electric and powerful. And the better you'll get at convincing an audience of your ideas or persuading them to act.

Even those without a ham bone in their bodies will come to anticipate a speaking engagement with a childlike giddiness. You'll look forward to it with pleasure. Having an impact on people is among the strongest natural drugs you'll ever know.

---

### The Agile Manager's Checklist

✔ Turn nervousness into energy that infuses the talk.
✔ Visualize the outcome of your speech—applause, congratuations on a job well done, people acting on your recommendations.
✔ If you make a mistake, carry on. Your audience will forgive you.
✔ Volunteer to make presentations. The more you do, the better you'll get.

*Chapter Six*

# Create a Strong Impact

In the conference room before the board, the Agile Manager had just finished his opening. The phrase "nothing less than the future of the company" hit them hard, he could tell.

Now he was explaining the product line: " . . . and that's a niche, I can assure you, that we can create and fill profitably." As he said the word profitably, he looked right in to the eyes of Morton, the banker. ("All he understands is financial statements," his boss had told him as he briefed him on the members of the board, "so be sure to use a lot of numbers in your talk." And be sure to talk directly to him when I do, the Agile Manager added to himself.)

Slow down, he cautioned himself. Start slowly and build. Rev up toward the end. He lowered his voice a notch. "And we are conservatively estimating the gross margin on this particular product at 56 percent." Again he looked into Morton's eyes, who raised his eyebrows and nodded back.

"And look at how clever it is," he continued. With a flourish, he pulled out a prototype and held it up high. As he placed it on top of the lectern, he locked eyes with Delores Ramirez, head of a local ad agency. "This is the kind of product advertisers dream about—you could fill a book with its benefits. Just for fun, I wrote *two single-spaced pages of benefits—and I could have gone on. I'll hand it out with some other things when I'm finished."* He smiled broadly and shifted his gaze to the CEO who nodded and smiled back.

*Just keep it up,* the Agile Manager said to himself. *Keep it up.*

If you do nothing more than what the preceding chapters suggest, you can still give a moving presentation. But as every effective speaker knows, there are many ways to increase the impact of a talk considerably.

Before we outline some of these methods, it should be said: You are a unique person with unique ways of moving people to action. Be wary of "borrowing" the mannerisms or techniques of another person. If you're a serious person, for instance, adding a few jokes you heard on the *Tonight Show* not only won't work for you but may detract from your message. Or slowing down to match the gravity of television preacher Robert Schuller when you're a high-energy type will only confuse an audience, especially one that knows you.

**Best Tip**

Don't borrow the mannerisms or techniques of another speaker. Be yourself.

Work to create your own "presentations personality." The more you are yourself, but amplified, the more effective you will be.

### Use Your Body to Speak

It's been said that words convey only 7 percent of your message when you're speaking. (Some studies put it at around 13 percent.) Your vocal variety, tone, body language, and visual aids convey the rest. Hearing that "fact" always makes me wonder: If you got up and moved around and grunted meaningfully but used no words, would the audience still get 93 percent of the message?

But that's not to minimize the importance of your movements and how you use your voice. These ingredients often make

ments and how you use your voice. These ingredients often make or break the presentation. People are watching them as closely as they are listening to your words.

**Best Tip**

Speak with your body as well as your voice.

Imagine you're telling people how to run a new tooling machine that's due to arrive in a week by standing stock-still at a lectern and reading from a paper. It's doubtful you'll teach people much, and you'll soon see a few heads nodding off. For a presentation on this topic, you'd want to be completely visible in front of the group, acting out movements and perhaps pointing to diagrams on a flip chart or overhead transparency.

**Your experiences and confidence animate the body.** It's best to use personal anecdotes and experiences in your talks whenever you can. You will unconsciously use gestures that not only inform but give your talk great credibility: "There I was in the foxhole, rain pouring down, when the sky lit up with tracers. Surprisingly, no attack came that night. But I had two revelations that dark, rainy night, and I'd like to share them with you . . ."

You'd begin this talk hunched down, perhaps pulling an imaginary poncho over your head, then gaze upward as the sky lit up. Your movements, completely authentic, would inform the audience that you were the genuine thing.

Your body language also conveys sincerity and the confidence you have in your words and yourself. If you watch people, especially business or government bureaucrats, the body often betrays insincerity when they speak. Say a CEO is explaining the reasons behind a restructuring that eliminates a thousand jobs from the company. He says, "I strongly believe that this is in the best interest of the company and will ensure we have a healthy future." But he's staring at a piece of paper as he says it, or looking over the heads of the listeners.

**Don't use body language self-consciously.** This is not to say that you should consciously construct a speech around movements intended to reinforce a message and sway an audience. If you have to stop and think about what you are doing, such movements and gestures will seem superficial. Dale Carnegie, in fact, said often that your goal is to forget all about gestures, movement, and vocal variety once you began a speech. If you've chosen the right topic, and "earned the right" to talk about it through experience or research, your gestures will arise naturally and convince even the most resistant audience. The point, he said, is to melt the inhibitions that keep you from expressing yourself with animation.

**Channel nervous energy.** Remember, you have nervous energy when you speak. It will come out somehow. If you don't channel it into a powerful speaking voice and gestures, it will come out in other ways: tightly clenched fists, fidgeting, quickly darting eyes, annoying pacing.

Look for opportunities to move and gesture. Usually these will seem obvious. If you're teaching a ground-school class in learning to fly, for instance, your hands will naturally grip an imaginary steering wheel, you'll flip imaginary switches, and your eyes will consult imaginary dials as though you were 8,000 feet in the air.

Use gestures to punctuate your words. It's a great way to emphasize key points.

Even if your talk is on a more abstract subject, use gestures to enliven it. If you want to make three quick points, for example, you can hold up your fingers to count them off.

**"Punctuate" your words.** Use gestures to punctuate your words. If your talk calls for you to say an emphatic "no," for example—"No, we will not do that! It's against the law!"—bang your right fist into your open left palm. Or hold your palms out toward the audience as if to say, "Stay away, evil person."

You can also use gestures to prompt people: "Who's ever had that experience?" you ask as you raise your arm to signal for a show of hands.

Some people have naturally elegant hand movements. They fluidly move their hands in circles, raise and lower them, or use them to underscore important words. If you have this ability, use it. It amplifies your message and helps convey meaning.

**Get out from behind the podium or lectern.** Even if you are giving a presentation on the most abstract subject imaginable, move around. But don't pace back and forth—the only speaker I ever saw who could pull that off was Tom Peters. Instead, pick a couple of points in the room and every so often walk to a new spot. Stay there a few minutes, then move to another. Some very effective speakers mingle with the audience by walking into an aisle, walking back to consult notes or turn a page on the flip chart, and moving around the room.

Moving around, even if it seems aimless to an audience, is far better than standing chained to a spot in the front of the room.

If you must stay close to the front of the room to tend to visual aids or for some other reason, move out so people can see your whole body. You have that much more opportunity to express yourself.

**Vary facial expressions.** Your face speaks volumes. Use it to convey or amplify meaning. Shake your head, roll your eyes, look heavenward, cast your eyes downward to show shame or remorse, watch an imaginary baseball sail over the left field fence, or whatever expression will tell part of a story.

With sincere, appropriate gestures, you can make us believe whatever you want. A friend once told me about going to see a master juggler perform whose bowling pins and other items had been lost by the airline company on his way in. Rather than call off the show, he juggled imaginary pins, fiery sticks, and knives. Before long, the audience could "see" these items; it oohed and ahed at just the right times and gave him a thunderous ovation at the end.

Here's an easy, effective way to see how people convey meaning with methods other than words: Watch a speaker or talk show on television with the sound turned off. Watch the face, movements, and gestures. You'll learn a lot.

### Use Vocal Variety

The audience also looks for sincerity, credibility, confidence, and meaning in your voice. The tone of your voice, for instance, is the foundation for words. If you say, "What I'm about to tell you will change your life" in a flat tone, no one will believe you. If you really believe that, you will say it with great gusto.

Here are some things to keep in mind as you rehearse:

- **Vary your tone.** Poor presenters speak in monotones or use just a few musical notes to convey their meaning. Excellent presenters use as many as twenty-five notes. Their voices rise when they are happy or excited, fall when they are sad, and become very low (to convey authority) when they want to impress a particular point on the audience.
- **Speak neither too quickly nor too slowly.** Speak in a range of 120 to 160 words a minute. (Record your voice and count if you need to.) People in the audience think at speeds of 200 words a minute or so, so if you speak slower than 120, they'll soon grow bored. On the other hand, if you speak faster than 150 or 160 words a minute, people won't have time to think about what your message means to them.
- **Pause every now and then.** Give people time to catch up with your thoughts by pausing. Pause just before or just after delivering an important thought.
- **Aim for a warm, natural tone.** You don't use a harsh or

negative tone with good friends, and for good reason. It would put them off. It puts off an audience, too. Ronald Reagan always drank warm water just before speaking; he said it relaxed his vocal cords and gave his voice a warmer tone. Ice water or sugary drinks like soda can tighten the vocal cords or otherwise gum them up. Avoid them.

- **Start slowly and build toward your conclusion.** No matter what you think about the activist Jesse Jackson, he gave a masterful speech at the 1996 Democratic Convention. He started off soft, low, and slow. That emphasized the reason in his words and the non-confrontational nature of the speech. Yet by the end he was his usual self—louder, and speaking faster in his trademark rhythmic cadence. The speech was forceful and moving.

- **Speak from the diaphragm.** Practice speaking from your gut. Those who speak from the vocal cords up tend to have thin, high voices. Power comes from the lungs, so breathe deeply and let the words rise from your chest cavity.

- **Vary the volume.** If you speak from the heart, you will naturally raise and lower your volume to match the message.

- **Lengthen or vary the pitch for a particular word.** "Now this point is soooooo important that I don't want you to miss it." Some speakers will say one word in a deliberately higher pitch to emphasize its importance.

In the last section I mentioned you could learn a lot by watching TV with the sound off. Now turn the sound on—but turn yourself around so you can't see the screen. How do people convey meaning with their vocal characteristics?

I find that stations of the Public Broadcasting Service the best place to conduct such experiments. They often televise presentations by people like the serious and rather sober spiritual guru Deepak Chopra, humorous fitness expert Covert Bailey, energetic motivational speaker Les Brown, moody consultant Tom Peters, and other experts. These are all effective speakers with very different styles. They set a good example by showing how effective you can be by being yourself.

### Be Enthusiastic

This is the prime ingredient for an effective speech. If you have chosen the right topic for your presentation, and if you are qualified to give it, you will have enthusiasm. It may, however, be hidden behind inhibitions.

Let it out. Enthusiasm overshadows many sins in public speaking and can turn a lackluster performance into a sterling one.

We've all seen average, unsophisticated, "ordinary people" on

**Best Tip**

Turn on a TV talk show, but don't look at the picture. How do speakers convey meaning through vocal variety?

talk shows like *Oprah Winfrey* give mini-presentations on emotional topics like what it's like to lose a child, where our school systems fail us, and so forth.

Even if the logic of their talk is flawed, even if they use ungrammatical language, and even if they can't make a concrete point, they move us.

They have something to say, and they use all their strength and enthusiasm to say it. And their point sometimes affects us profoundly. There's a lesson in there for all of us.

With the proper amount of enthusiasm for your topic, you can make most people believe just about anything. (Proof? Adolph Hitler.) An enthusiastic speaker can make a lifelong smoker swear off cigarettes, a couch potato go out and run, or a tired workforce return to the job with renewed energy and commitment.

When you combine enthusiasm with a strong, clear message, good organization, and preparation, you can take over the world. And enthusiasm needn't be effusive and sloppy—it can be controlled power that motivates you. At root, enthusiasm is a reflection of the energy with which you believe what you're saying. That energy can take many forms.

## Be Humble

All effective speakers have something in common: They have strained out any hint of arrogance from their talks. They are, as a rule, humble. It is, they know, the only way to have an impact on others. It's only when people believe you're on the same plane with them that they accept your message.

The arrogant convey the attitude that they are smarter than others, or that the audience is stupid. Many managers with inflated egos diminish the impact they could have on people by appearing to believe themselves above their subordinates.

> **Best Tip**
>
> Learn to speak without notes. It's not that hard, and people will assume you're brilliant.

Include yourself in the examples you use. If you're speaking about the need to adopt new methods at work, for instance, it's helpful to say to the audience, honestly, that "I know how hard this is going to be. I'm sure I'll slip back into the old methods upon occasion, and I'll need you good folks to help keep me on track." Acknowledging your own difficulties with a policy or situation goes a long way toward humanizing yourself and helping others accept what you have to say.

## Try Speaking from Memory

Never memorize a speech. If you get lost in the middle of a memorized speech, it can be hard to find your way again. Worse, a memorized speech has a "canned" quality that diminishes the impact on an audience.

But speaking without notes or an outline has a remarkable effect on an audience. A friend heard the management expert Rosabeth Moss Kanter speak for an hour on world trade. Her seatmates were astonished—Kanter used no notes! What a brilliant person!

Well, she is brilliant. But speaking without notes doesn't take brilliance. You can do it, too. You do that by creating a series of images you use as memory "pegs," and then hanging your notes or outline upon them.

Create an image for each of the numbers one through ten. Make it personal. For instance, one is the apple tree in the back yard. Two is the Honda. Three is a favorite mug. And so on.

Learn to use these memory pegs by first remembering shopping lists. Let's say you need a cabbage, bag of coffee, and gallon of milk. Take your first image—the apple tree—and picture it with cabbages hanging from the branches instead of apples. Then think of coffee beans filling the interior of your Honda. Then imagine a gallon of milk teetering precariously on top of your mug.

The zanier the picture, the better it will stick in your memory.

After you get the hang of the system, use it to remember the main points of a speech. Point one: Research at the University of Chicago suggests this will be a growing market in the next century. Point two: The sales of two key products also predicts a new market. Point three: Consolidated Box company is already getting into it.

Imagine the researchers in white lab coats that say "UC" hanging from the apple tree. Imagine yourself crammed into the Honda with the two products. Imagine looking into your mug and finding it filled with Consolidated Box logos.

### Look Great

Like it or not, people do judge a book by its cover. The way you look adds to your credibility. That's why nattily dressed nasty people sometimes get far before they are exposed.

The rule of thumb is to dress as well as the best-dressed person in the audience will be. For anything but a small in-house presentation, that usually means a suit for men and appropriate professional clothing for women.

Pay for top-notch clothing. It makes a difference.

The audience, mind you, won't concentrate on your clothes and appearance. It will simply do a quick mental check to ensure that you look the part. If you're a CEO, it will look for the carefully coifed hair, the gray or blue suit, the carefully trimmed nails, and so forth.

If you're a research scientist, it will look for the beard, the glasses, and perhaps the pocket protector and a row of pens.

Sometimes you can get away with looking like something other than the part, but only for a good reason. Ben & Jerry's chairman Ben Cohen, for instance, hardly looks like the millionaire chairman of a multimillion dollar company. Yet he represents perfectly the ice-cream firm's countercultural spirit. He's a walking marketing statement.

Once people check you out, they forget about your appearance and concentrate on your message.

### Maintain Eye Contact

The best speakers look you in the eye. An audience knows that a speaker who doesn't look you in the eye may have something to hide. Or may lack confidence in the message. Either way, the effect is bad.

And don't look *at* somebody. Look into their eyes and make a connection. Don't hold it too long; you don't want to intimidate or make people uncomfortable. Hold your gaze long enough that the person knows you are speaking directly to him or her.

Hold your gaze long enough to let a person know you are speaking directly to him or her.

Maintaining eye contact helps the audience feel included. Remember, you're really having a conversation—but with ten or a hundred people, not two or three.

Eye contact also has a way of baring your soul to people. You say to an audience, "I'm letting you see me, warts and all, today.

My eyes tell you that I believe what I am saying."

Veteran speakers also occasionally speak directly to people who appear to be hostile. It's a way of saying, "I'm not afraid of you, and I'll do my best to answer your concerns."

Don't bother trying to make eye contact with those who don't appear to be listening or who look bored. But bear in mind you

Don't assume someone with a bored look on his face has tuned you out.

never really know what's going on in someone's mind. I've thought certain people were totally tuned out at my talks. Then they come up afterwards to ask me pointed questions that showed they listened carefully. (And some who lock eyes with you and smile gaily are thinking of the novel they can't wait to return to that evening.)

If someone refuses to look at you or otherwise exhibits negative body language, ignore it. You don't know the exact cause. If someone suddenly scowls, it may be because she just realized she forgot to do something important. Another may look pained due to indigestion, not your words.

### Banish Ums and Ahs

Nothing detracts from a talk as when you constantly fall back on ums and ahs. We all do it occasionally, but once in a while you'll hear a speaker who can't say a sentence without inserting an "um" between every half-sentence. It's painful to sit through.

Same goes for phrases like "you know." I once heard the actor Woody Harrelson speak on a topic dear to him, the environment. But I soon cared little about his views, because he turned them into mush with the ten or twelve "you knows" he uttered every minute.

Most Toastmasters chapters have a "Wizard of Ahs" who counts the number of times you say um or ah. At our club, you get fined a nickel an "um." At other chapters, a member drops a Ping-Pong ball into a bucket every time you say um. Such methods soon make you aware of how frequently you use verbal crutches.

### Interact with the Audience

You can keep an audience interested and on its toes by interacting with it. Here's how:

- Ask questions. For example, "How many of you have been robbed?"
- Ask for a vote. "I can go two directions here—I can talk about reengineering order fulfillment or product development. Which would you prefer?"
- Ask for volunteers. "OK, now to show you how easy it will be to run this video camera, I need someone to come up and act as guinea pig." Someone usually will.
- You can even single people out in the audience and ask questions or have them speak about something. But be careful here. You must appear to have perfectly good intentions—i.e., people must feel you're not going to ridicule them. A friendly demeanor helps, as does a sharp eye as to who might respond favorably.
- If someone asks a question you can't answer, and it's appropriate, you might throw it out to the audience:"Gee I don't know. Does anybody here know the answer to that?"

Interacting with an audience is unpredictable, so be prepared to think on your feet if things don't go as planned. If you know you're going to ask a question or for volunteers, think about what could go wrong and have an escape route planned.

### Maintain a Friendly Demeanor; Smile

Roman orator Cicero maintained that a speaker's job was to delight the audience. If the subject is right and you're the right person, delight people.

Delighting people isn't always appropriate, of course. If you're delivering bad news, a sober delivery is probably called for. If you're mad and ready to kick butt, laughs and jokes won't do the job.

But when you can, delight by smiling and laughing often, and by appearing easygoing. Those with a friendly manner, I've found, are the most versatile speakers. People take to them right from the start, stay with

After a presentation, evaluate your job. What worked? What didn't?

them, and are more than ready to adopt a change or take action.

The problem is, the easygoing, friendly Alan Alda–type personality doesn't fit all of us. It doesn't fit me, for instance. As a result, I stay within my abilities and don't do lighthearted or humorous speeches that would require that particular persona.

You'll find that the audience is like a mirror. If they sit grim-faced and clenched, it's probably because that's the image you are projecting. If the audience laughs and shows animation, it's because you are.

Smile often. It's a lubricant between you and the audience that greases acceptance of your message.

### Evaluate Yourself

After presentations, skilled speakers ask themselves: "What worked? What didn't? Did I get the weight of my message across? Did the audience understand clearly what I said? Could I have said it better or more forcefully? Was it the right message for the audience? When did they tune out? When did they listen? Were the stories and facts the right ones to use?" There's little you can't analyze profitably.

If possible, get someone in the audience you trust to tell you how you and your presentation came across. Communications expert Bert Decker suggests a "3 X 3" evaluation. Ask your friend to name three strengths in your talk and three distractions.

You can even ask the audience how you did. Hand out a one-page evaluation form before you end and ask people to take two minutes to fill it out for you.

Another plug for Toastmasters: Each speech you do is evaluated in depth by another, experienced club member. And many others will comment on your presentations when you are done. One speech at Toastmasters can reveal more about your impact than five done "on the outside" where people will be reticent about delivering criticism.

However you accomplish it, there's no quicker way to learn effective speaking than through constructive evaluations.

---

### The Agile Manager's Checklist

✔ Let the message animate your body. It can tell as much of the story as your words can.

✔ Get out from behind the lectern or podium. Interact.

✔ Pause now and then. It gives the audience time to catch up.

✔ Strain out any hint of arrogance from your talk. If you don't, you'll lose the audience.

✔ Your audience wants you to look a certain way. Don't disappoint it.

✔ Smile!

# Chapter Seven

# Use Visual Aids Effectively

The Agile Manager pointed to the easel with his retractable pointer. "You can see the difference right there. Look at it!" *Throttle back slightly,* he thought to himself. *Don't become bombastic.*

All eyes on the room focused on the pie chart showing market share. He'd done two charts, both in color to show contrast better. The one on top showed overall market share in medical instrumentation without the new product line. The one on the bottom showed market share with it. In the second, the company's market share was half again as big. It'd taken bites out of the shares of all the other companies, but especially that of Murphy Technology.

The Agile Manager didn't point that out directly, but he thought he could see a couple of the managers eyeing Murphy's slice of the pie. There was no love lost between the two companies; the rivalry had been bitter for the better part of ten years.

"And this," he said abruptly, flipping the page. His pointer thwacked the paper. It landed on a column chart showing company revenue versus its competitors. Once again, it showed revenue with the new product line, and then without it. He liked this chart. It showed at a glance how the gain for the company bit into Murphy's revenues—and when, for the first time, the company's *revenue exceeded Murphy's. That would be a real milestone.*

*Morton, the banker, pursed his lips and seemed about to talk. Time for that later, thought the Agile Manager. But be prepared. The boss said Morton hates pie-in-the-sky figures and will try to pick them apart.*

*"And finally this . . ." said the Agile Manager, moving quickly to stall Morton.*

A good visual aid is a valuable, often essential, adjunct to a presentation. But before we outline the ways you can augment your talk using visual aids, note well: You can give a marvelous presentation with no visual aids whatsoever. You can paint vivid pictures with your words and gestures that will live on for weeks in the minds of your listeners.

## Best Tip

You can give an excellent presentation or speech using no visual aids whatsoever.

You can help people picture your point by creating "invisible" visuals. For example, say you're describing how far each planet is from the next. You walk to one end of the room. "Here's the Sun," you say. You take a few steps. "Here's Mercury." A few steps more. "Venus." "The Earth," and so on. People will see the relative scale without trouble.

Or imagine you're describing a new assembly-line setup. You have a few chairs ready to move around. Grabbing one and placing it down, you say, "Here's the initial parts station." You plop down another one. "Here's where you put together gizmo A and gizmo B." Another chair, which now, with the others, takes on a horseshoe shape. "A different worker takes the gizmos and screws them together. He then adds a harness for both and passes it on to the third worker." You grab the last chair. "That person does a quick quality check, packs it, and puts it onto a conveyor belt that goes to the shipping area."

You could describe the same scene without the chairs by moving around the room. Either way, people are imagining the assembly line quite vividly.

### Caution!

First, visual aids can become a crutch that handicaps your presentation. If you have fifty slides or transparencies, for example, you can stand in the dark and let your visuals do the talking for you. But the presentation won't be nearly as effective as when you throw yourself into it.

Second, some people spend far too much time creating sophisticated visual aids. Unfortunately, sometimes it's part of the company culture to spend as much time on how you present information as you do on gathering good information to present.

Make your charts and graphs good enough to do the job. A black and white transparency shows profit figures as well as a Technicolor slide. (If your company values slickness over content, consider finding another job.)

### Types of Visual Aids

Any visual aid should augment your message, not make it. And it should fit your talk exactly. If you're pointing out items on a balance sheet projected on a wall, and you show the income statement along with it, you'll create confusion. Or if your talk centers on an airplane's fuselage and all your diagrams include the whole plane, you're offering too much. Let your visual aids support your points and arguments and attempt no more.

Among your choices for visual aids:

**Props.** These are among the best because they are the most vivid. If you can hold up or point to a three-dimensional object, you'll impress people. For instance, if you're discussing a new version of a product, show a prototype. Designers (like architects or shipbuilders) often make scale models of the item they've designed.

Some experts suggest using props no matter what for dramatic effect. For instance, if you're talking about the need to be observant in the marketplace, you hold up a giant pair of glasses. Or if you're talking about the company's ultimate goal, you hold up a miniature version of a soccer goal or hockey net to show the importance of focusing on the end.

I would rather use words to help an audience picture such a broad point. Some listeners, however, process concrete visual images better than words, so keep the suggestion in mind.

**Flip charts and white boards.** These are useful for working discussions and informational presentations. For example, if you're describing a formula for getting a useful result, nothing beats a working demonstration. It helps show the audience the process you're going through to obtain a particular result.

Also, use flip charts or white boards when you're taking audience input: "How many ways are there to ship a box?" Or, "How many ways can Product X be useful to people?"

You can also use a flip chart or white board to underscore the points you are making and keep the thread of your argument visible to all. For example, say you're arguing for a new facility. As you speak, you write down the main points one by one. At the end of the presentation, all the points are visible to the audience, making your case—you hope—irresistible:

```
— More space for two new fabricators

— Production per square foot increases

— Space around perimeter for six small offices

— Eliminates need for warehouse in Johnstown

— Better layout for just-in-time deliveries

— Closer to key vendors

— Cuts truck-docking time in half
```

Make sure your chart or board can be seen by everyone in the room. Walk around the room beforehand to make sure. When working at a flip chart or board, never turn your back to the audience, and never block the board from sight. Write big, and be sure you know how to spell all the words you're writing. A misspelled word gets uglier and more distracting as time goes on.

Practice turning the pages on the flip chart. It's not as easy as it looks, especially while you are talking to an audience.

Use different colored markers if it helps you make a point or differentiate among them. Stick to those, however, that will show up well, like blue, green, red, or purple.

**Transparencies (overhead or slides).** These, especially overhead transparencies, are the workhorses of most presentations. They offer a counterpoint to your words and another way for the audience to absorb your meaning. You can also create neat, legible visuals before your talk, a big advantage if you have poor handwriting. (And pre-drawn visuals can serve as your notes by outlining key points.)

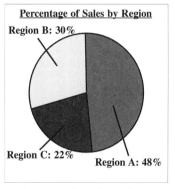

Turn numbers into charts whenever you can.

If you're offering any kind of financial data, use transparencies. If you can turn numbers into a chart or graph of some sort, do so. The audience will get the point sooner and with greater impact.

Same goes for anything you can diagram. For example, rather than list the sites where you make furniture, show a map with a big dot where each plant is. Instead of listing each key part to a product, create a diagram with arrows pointing to each. Rather than listing sales territories in the form of a list of states, show the country and color code each territory.

Present no more than one idea at a time on a transparency. That doesn't necessarily mean no more than one point. A slide may have one idea—why we need a new company jet—and then offer three reasons that support your contention.

If you have a transparency that lists a number of items you are going to talk about, keep a sheet of paper over those you haven't mentioned yet. Otherwise your audience will jump ahead and think about what you are going to say rather than what you're saying.

Sometimes an outline keeps the audience focused. You can create an outline of the items you are discussing, with a big arrow by the one you're discussing at the moment. With this type of aid, no one says, "Now where are we? I've forgotten."

```
            Need for three new hires
            Who will supervise them
            Where we'll put them
   ➡       What we'll pay them
            What we'll expect from them
            How they will impact financial results
```

Use large type with plenty of space between lines. You want the words legible from a distance. To that end, avoid fancy typefaces. Stick with the simple.

Last, buy a good presentations software program and learn how to use it. Once you get the hang of it, it makes creating graphics for your presentations easy. Popular programs include Adobe Persuasion and Microsoft's PowerPoint.

Connected to a laptop computer and projected on a big screen, these programs can help you create an exciting, dynamic presentation without undue effort.

**Multimedia.** Multimedia presentations generally bore me. Why have a speaker if he or she simply punches a button and lets the computer do the talking? At the very least, don't believe those who want to sell you the ability to create such presentations when they say that this is how people want to be spoken to nowadays. They don't. People get enough rushing images and sound at home when they watch television commercials. A live human being with an effectively told message will beat a machine any day.

OK, I'm sure there are appropriate times for creating multimedia presentations. Just don't eliminate the human element. It's far too valuable.

**Best Tip**

Don't stage a multimedia presentation just because you can. Do it because it's the best way to present material.

**Computer-generated visuals.** Sometimes having a computer image projected on a screen or wall can come in handy. For instance, imagine you are describing different budget scenarios at a marketing department meeting. You could project a spreadsheet for all to see, then change figures as you describe "what if" situations. "Here's what happens to the contribution margin if we spend an additional $150,000 on space advertising." Or, "If manufacturing got the gross margin on the product up to 50 percent, look at how much extra money we would have to work with."

Computers can be unstable, as you know, so be sure you have a reliable power supply and enough RAM to handle what you're doing. Also, don't forget that if you put your thumb in the wrong place you can wipe out your presentation. Imagine what could go wrong with the presentation and be ready to deal with glitches. (Know how to use the program inside and out, too. You want to be ready if the boss throws something at you like, "That's very interesting, Mary. But what happens to the bottom line if we take product returns of 11 percent?")

**Handouts.** If you want to leave the audience with a few important thoughts, give people a handout that summarizes your talk or somehow adds a dimension to it. Hand out the paper after you speak, though, otherwise people will stare at it rather than you. And keep it to one page, unless there's a good reason to offer more.

One advantage of handouts: You can offer more detail than

you can in a talk. In a presentation I gave on the value of exercising, I spent most of the time explaining the benefits. At the end I passed out a paper that contained three sample exercise programs. Had I described them or put them on a flip chart, who would have taken the time to write them down?

### Avoid Technical Problems

Whenever you use audiovisual equipment, check it out before your presentation. See how your overhead transparencies and slides appear on it. See where cords cross your path. Have extra bulbs handy and know how to insert them. Anticipate problems and how you would deal with them. It'll save you embarrassment if you have to solve a problem standing before thirty people.

---

**The Agile Manager's Checklist**

✔ Don't let visual aids become a crutch that impairs your presentation.

✔ Use props when you can. They are the most vivid visual aids.

✔ Use a whiteboard or flip chart to keep you (and the audience) organized.

✔ Offer a handout when it usefully augments your talk.

✔ Test audiovisual equipment before the talk.

# Special Speaking Situations

*"The man who sees both sides of a question is a
man who sees absolutely nothing at all."*

OSCAR WILDE

*Chapter Eight*

# Handle
# Questions and Answers

Morton, the banker, cast a wary eye at the Agile Manager. "Young man," he said. "You make some curious suppositions about sales revenues for this new line of products. Where do the figures come from?"

"Thank you for that excellent question, sir," said the Agile Manager, leaning forward with his hands on the table. "I can see how you might wonder about the revenue projections.

"How we arrived at those figures is complicated. Basically, the financial people took historical figures for every product the company has ever produced and looked for parallels among them and the ones we have in development. They looked at the market, price, extent of distribution, and so forth. Meanwhile, the marketing people took a probable budget and estimated what ad campaigns, trade shows, and direct marketing would do for the product—"

"Yes, I understand all that. But you show us pie charts and bar graphs and whatnot that show what appear to be real revenues and real market share, but the figures are guesses. Am I right?"

"Of course." *My former wife kept the crystal ball, sir,* thought the Agile Manager. "That's the best we—or anyone—can do. But I can assure you that some of the best minds in the company worked on projecting revenues."

*"Thank you. That's all I wanted to hear," said Morton. Some of the other directors glanced at him coldly; what was the point of all that?*

*The CEO cleared his throat and said, "I would like to see your methodology for coming up with those figures."*

*"Of course, sir. I'll have a short report ready for you by 9:00 tomorrow morning. Yes?" He looked at Ramirez, the ad lady.*

*"Can you explain again briefly how the smaller version is suited for the trauma market?" Thank you!*

*"Yes," he said brightly. "You see, in emergency situations . . ."*

Many presentations have a question-and-answer session at the end. These can be trying for the speaker, who's usually ready to leave the lectern at that point.

Q&A sessions are nerve-wracking because they are unpredictable. What if somebody is hostile? How do I cut off people who babble on, unable to ask a simple question? What if a peer—or worse, a superior—tries to embarrass me?

Once again, the key to handling Q&A sessions is planning. Plus a few tricks to maintain a degree of control.

> ## *B*est *T*ip
>
> Figure out ahead of time how you'll answer tough, even hostile, questions.

### Prepare for Tough Questions

As part of your preparation for the presentation, set aside half an hour to imagine all the questions you are going to get. Formulate answers to them. Most important, be ready to answer the questions you *don't* want to get ("How come your job isn't being cut along with ours?" Or, "What about the arsenic-laced cesspool beyond the truck garage?").

Your audience, collectively, will be smart. They will probably ask good, pointed questions. Be your own best critic and prepare for them.

### Q&A Basics

Follow these guidelines for a successful question-and-answer session:

**Set a time limit.** Before you begin, say something like, "I've got ten minutes now to take a few questions." Then adhere to the time limit you set. Having a time limit helps people focus their questions, and it gives you a legitimate out when you've reached the limit. Otherwise the session goes on and on, deteriorating all the while.

**Best Tip**

If nobody wants to be the first to ask a question, ask one of yourself: "One thing you may be wondering is how I . . ."

**Move closer to the audience.** Ideally, Q&A sessions are more intimate than the speech or presentation you just gave. If you're standing behind a podium or lectern or table, move out in front of it, or go into the audience in the manner of a Phil Donahue. Doing so helps relax both an audience and you.

**Have a few questions ready to get things started.** Experienced speakers will often have a few friends in the audience ready with softball—easy—questions to get things moving positively. Or they may ask questions the speaker wants to address. You can also ask yourself questions if no one is forthcoming: "I'm sure one question on your minds is probably this: How do I collect severance benefits if I'm laid off?" Once someone—even you—asks the first question, people loosen up and begin asking their own.

**Use questions to repeat or amplify important points.** Always do your best to answer the question that's asked—no one likes the politician who can't give a straight answer to an honest question. That said, take advantage of opportunities to use an answer to hammer home important points you made in your speech: " . . . and that takes me back to my original point: wearing a helmet on the job can save your life."

Also, sometimes you have an opportunity to slip in something you forgot: "Yes, I think you're absolutely right, John. By the way, I forgot to mention that the metal housing of these units is an eighth of an inch thick. It can withstand all the punishment we give it."

**If you don't know, say so.** If you don't know the answer to a question, admit it. If the answer is easy to find out, promise to get back to the person. (With a large group, or with people you don't know, ask the questioner to slip you a business card after the talk so you can respond.)

**Trust yourself to answer the question.** Speech expert Bert Decker, in his book *You've Got to Be Believed to Be Heard*, makes a good point: Don't censor yourself as you answer questions. Trust your gut and let the words flow. You'll seem—and be— much more believable.

**Listen hard for the question being asked.** Many people find it difficult to ask a simple, clear question. You sometimes have to strain to understand what's being asked. If in doubt, say something like, "What I think I hear you asking is whether or not there's a chance the plant will reopen before Christmas. Is that correct?"

**Make sure you answer the question.** If in doubt, ask for confirmation: "Does that answer the question?" Q&A sessions are important events for building credibility and validating all the good points you made in your speech. If you seem slippery or evasive, you may damage the work you did up to that point.

**Disarm the long winded.** Some people don't ask questions. They seek a platform to espouse their own ideas. The rest of the group will thank you when you break in and say, "Have you got a question for me?" Others are unable to come to the point. Interrupt them, if necessary, and say, "I think what you're leading up to is this: Have we got any R&D money left over for Product X? The answer is no, and here's why." If possible, don't give the speaker an opportunity to break in again to "clarify" your question. After answering the question, take another, immediately, from a different side of the room.

### Dealing with Hostile Questioners

At some time or other, you'll face a hostile questioner. Sometimes questioners are passionate about a subject and listen closely for any little nuance that goes against what they know or believe. And then there's that breed of person who delights in needling speakers. Rather than wish either sort away, prepare for them.

First thing to remember: Never argue with a questioner. You can't win.

If possible, find something to agree on. For example, before you answer a tough question, say something like, "Thanks for that question. My daughter is also in the third grade, and I know how mad I get when the evaluations she gets from teachers are incomplete or not rigorous enough. Here's how I feel about the subject: . . ."

Avoid using the word "but," as in, "I agree that time off around the holidays is important, but we have a plant to run and product to get out." Smart audiences know to discount everything before the "but." They can also hear the snide undertone. Better: "I agree that time off around the holidays is important. And I also know that we have to keep the

Never argue with a questioner. You can't win.

pipeline filled with product. We're trying to maintain a balance—keeping you happy as well as our customers."

It's especially important to ensure you've answered the question posed by someone obviously upset or angry. If you don't, that person can poison the thinking of others in the audience.

"See, I told you she never gives a straight answer about anything."

Sometimes you just can't win with a person. Usually, the rest of the audience recognizes the truly hostile or illogical questioner and is on your side. Get out from under the tirade with grace: "I respect your right to disagree with me on this issue." Or, "Thanks for your thoughts." Then take another question immediately.

Eventually, you'll learn to look forward to a good Q&A session. Nothing cements a talk as well. It wraps up the presentation for both you and the audience, and it helps ensure that it did the job intended to the satisfaction of all.

## The Agile Manager's Checklist

✔ Plan to handle questions at the end of your presentation. It's an opportunity for both you and the audience to continue learning.
✔ Move closer to the audience for the Q&A session.
✔ Don't be afraid to say, "I don't know." Be quick to add, "I'll find out for you."
✔ Prepare for hostile questions and needlers.

# Chapter Nine

# *H*andle Difficult Situations with Aplomb

*The Agile Manager leaned back in his chair, feet on the desk, unwinding from the presentation. The telephone buzzed.*

*"Fantastic talk," said the man with the Texas twang. "The CEO called me special to say what a great job you did. You won them all over."*

*"Thanks!" said the smiling Agile Manager.*

*"He also said you did a great job handling Morton—you were respectful while holding your ground. That's not easy to do."*

*"I was ready for him, I guess."*

*"Anyway, you did such a good job that you're gonna have to do it again, but this time for all the managers in the division— about thirty-five people. I've blocked out an hour in the big presentation room three weeks from tomorrow at 10:00 A.M. This'll be our roll-out session for the troops. I'll talk for about ten minutes to lead off, and the CEO will pop in to have a few words at the very end. You'll be in the middle, outlining the product line and our development and manufacturing strategies. I figure you'll need an hour, maybe a bit more. You up to it?"*

*"Of course."*

*No rest for the wicked, thought the Agile Manager as he sighed and pulled out his clipboard to plan the event. Let's see, fifteen minutes on the overview, ten minutes to show the video that marketing produced, another fifteen minutes to describe the manufacturing flow . . .*

Three speaking situations challenge even experienced speakers: Longer presentations, impromptu speaking, and introductions.

### Keep the Audience Tuned in to Longer Presentations

Beware the longer speech or presentation. No matter what the subject, the audience begins losing interest after forty-five minutes or so.

This guideline is for mere mortals like us. I've seen Tom Peters hold an audience mesmerized for two hours, and all he did was stalk, talking into a microphone, from one end of the stage to the other. No visuals, no notes. Star power may have something to do with the effect he got. Likewise, Harvard Business School professor and leadership expert John Kotter kept me spellbound for two hours—but he introduced an occasional video or audio clip.

Sometimes long presentations are necessary and beneficial, such as when you have a good deal of information to convey or when you conduct training or a seminar.

> **Best Tip**
>
> After thirty or forty minutes, do something different. Show a film, ask for questions, or give the audience a break.

Delivering a longer speech or presentation isn't all that different from giving a short one. All that we've discussed so far pertains to both. The main difference, however, is that you must be aware of when the audience reaches its tolerance or saturation point.

First, understand that the attention span of most people has a limit. One study showed that this limit is seventeen minutes.

Therefore, every twenty minutes or so, change the subject.

Second, summarize and review your message often. Remind the audience where you've been, and where you are going.

Third, after the first thirty or forty minutes, do something different. Continue to do something different every ten to fifteen minutes. Stop for questions, invite audience participation, show a short film, give the audience an exercise to do, offer a break or something to eat, and so forth.

Think of the longer presentation in terms of segments. Make each a gem.

In short, unless you are an extraordinary person who has had extraordinary experiences, don't even think about talking at an audience for two hours. Think in terms of segments, and make each a polished, interesting gem.

### Impromptu Speaking

It happens. You're at a testimonial dinner or breakfast meeting, and the host or toastmaster says, "You know, we haven't heard from Jill yet. How about coming up and saying a few words, Jill?" Or the CEO says, "Jack, I know you've got just the expertise I'm talking about. Why don't you come up and explain the process for everybody?" Here's how to handle it:

**When you know the subject cold.** If, as in the last question, you get a pointed request about something you know, relax. You can do it in your sleep. And remember, in most impromptu speaking situations, you won't be expected to speak long.

As you go to the front of the room, think of the one point you want to make. It could be "The importance of volunteers to the organization" or "How we at Acme Company turn resins into plastic baseball bats," or "Fertile ground for our next marketing effort."

Then think of an example that illustrates that point. This could be easy:

Before the meeting today, I ran into Jim Thomas in the hallway. He told me about visiting the nursing home on North Street the night before to help the residents and employees of the home put up holiday decorations and sing a few carols. Jim said it brought a tear to his eye to listen to them all sing 'Silent Night.'

Jim feels he got his reward for participating in that event by simply hearing a timeless song beautifully sung. But his reward, I feel, goes much deeper than that. By showing he cares, he knows he is making life easier, if only a little bit, for people who don't have much longer to live.

That reward extends to our organization as a whole. And if it weren't for all you dedicated, selfless volunteers . . .

Remember, if you tell an experience or anecdote that happened to you, you will add enthusiasm, authenticity, and action to your impromptu speech that will enliven it and impress your listeners.

**When you are asked to "say a few words."** If you're asked to say a few words about nothing in particular, you have to pull something out of your hat fast. If you don't, it could be embarrassing.

Fortunately, you can be "prepared" to speak impromptu. You make a point, tie it to an incident or example, and be seated.

The easiest way to think of something to say is to ask yourself, why am I here at this function? Maybe the purpose of the meeting is to discuss the importance of opening the South American market. In that case you can amplify the theme:

I was in my son Darien's room the other night. On one wall he has a huge map of the world. I focused on the South American continent. I looked at each country one by one—Uruguay, Brazil, Peru, Colombia, and the rest—and realized how little I knew about each. Then I looked at Chile and was shocked. The map was wrong! It showed Chile on the west coast of South America, instead of the east coast!

I was wrong, of course, not the map. My ignorance made me pledge that night—and I renew that pledge right now—to study South America through books and visits until I know it as well as any Yanqui can, study it until we can begin working with partners down there and eventually understand its people well enough to supply it with products that make their lives easier . . .

Maybe the purpose of the event is to honor a retiree. Again, an easy call:

> I first met Ralph Hjallberg in 1978. I can still remember the day. It was in late October around the World Series, and I had a Yankees jacket on. He stood in front of the door and said, stonefaced, "You're not coming in here with that on." Remember, I didn't even know this guy! "Not only that," he continued, "But if I see you wearing it again I'll dock you an hour's pay." He stared at me for another ten seconds or so, then broke into a huge grin and said, "Welcome Mr. Satterly. We've been looking forward to your arrival since last May."
>
> Ralph's humor is one of many things that have meant so much to Value Grade Corporation over the past twenty-five years . . .

**Learn to buy time**. Experienced extemporaneous speakers learn how to buy time by stalling, but imperceptibly. If you need time to formulate an answer, say, "Thank you for asking me to speak on such an interesting question, Linda. Not too long ago, I had a long drive to a client's office that gave me an opportunity to think about that very subject, and quite a bit else, too. It was a glorious day, and I stopped along the coast to dip my feet into the water—but never mind about that. As for the question . . ." By the time you're done with that preamble, your unconscious mind will most likely miraculously hand you something sensible to say.

**Best Tip**

Just for fun: Whenever you're at a function, imagine what you would say if called upon to go up to the podium.

**Refer to the audience.** It's hard to fail if you somehow include the audience. Single out someone for praise, tell a story, praise the group as a whole, and show why you're proud to be a member of such an excellent organization.

You can train yourself to speak impromptu two ways:

- *Play what-if.* As Dale Carnegie wrote, a good way to prepare for being called upon to speak impromptu is to ask yourself, while you're sitting in the audience or around a banquet table, "What would I say if I were suddenly called upon to utter a few words?" Ninety-nine times out of a hundred you won't be. But that exercise will seem a good investment of time when a friend or associate taps you on the shoulder and asks you to step up to the microphone.
- *Play table topics.* Another way to prepare for impromptu speaking is to play, frequently, a game with your friends or family around the dinner table. It's simple: You give one of your table mates a subject, and he or she talks about it for a minute or two. Then someone asks you a question, and so on until you've gone around the table.

Questions can be on current events, morals or values, likes or dislikes, or just about anything.

The whole point is to learn to think on your feet, especially when asked a question about which you know nothing.

*Best Tip*

Play a game around the dinner table: One person names a topic, and another person has to speak on it for ninety seconds.

When you are the questioner, strive to ask questions that require answers beyond a few words. The person answering should be able to speak for a good ninety seconds. And when you are the one answering, do your best to make a coherent point and end with strength, just as you would in a speech.

The game teaches you to be inventive with answers. For instance, you learn the perfectly acceptable technique of avoiding answering a question you know nothing about and answering instead one of your own choosing. For example: "The worst car I ever owned? I've loved every car I've ever owned. Each has been a brand-new Mercedes, except for the month I tried a Rolls. Didn't like it. Actually, I don't drive. But I do know that

you use a car for transportation. You also use a bicycle ᵢᵤ_
portation.

"Let me tell you about a harrowing experience I had riding a
mountain bike last winter . . ."

### Introductions

A bad introduction can ruin a
great speech. I heard about a host
who introduced an after-dinner
speaker this way: "Well, here we
are at the moment you've all been
waiting for. We tried to get Bruce

**Best Tip**

If you're introducing a
speaker, take time to do it
right. Sell the message and
the person delivering it.

Smith to talk this evening, but he wasn't available. Bruce sug-
gested Marnie Lynn, but she also had something to do. So instead we got Tom Higbee, who's going to talk about . . ." The
host ruffled through some notes. ". . . I'm not sure what. Let's
welcome Tom Higbee." The response, as you can imagine was
tepid—and grossly unfair to the speaker.

When you introduce a speaker, sell the message and the person. People need to know why *this* speaker is talking on *this*
subject to *them*.

To introduce someone properly,

**1. Explain the subject the speaker is about to discuss.**
"Tony is here to talk about the new ISO standards for industrial
adhesives."

**2. Explain why the subject concerns the audience.** "All
we do around here, as you know, is manufacture adhesives. The
ISO standards are an important way we can maintain quality
and do the work as efficiently as possible. Equally important,
ISO certification is a stamp of approval that can open up markets in other parts of the world to us. In effect, it says, 'These
guys know what they are doing. You can be assured of quality
adhesives.' And if we can open up new markets, maybe we can
hang onto our jobs for a while longer."

**3. Explain the qualifications of the speaker.** "Tony has studied manufacturing techniques since his early days at Cal Tech. He went on to get a masters in Materials Technology at MIT. After that, he joined a Coopers & Smith consulting unit, which sent him to Germany to learn about our industry.

"Still a consultant with Coopers & Smith, Tony has helped thirty-five companies achieve ISO certification in manufacturing adhesives. We're lucky to have him here today, because he's about to spend a year in Saudi Arabia. Ladies and Gentleman, Tony Schwartzbach!"

Give the person you introduce a good send-off by saying the name loud and with enthusiasm.

If someone fails to introduce you properly (the rule rather than the exception), be ready to do it yourself. Here's a good example:

> The purpose of my speech is to show you how organizing into self-managing teams can boost manufacturing productivity by 4 to 6 percent. These are averages of results I've helped companies achieve in their own plants. Some, like Murphy Technology, achieved productivity improvements on the order of 10 percent.
>
> My background is in organizational behavior. I learned much of what I know from Dr. Lindsey Cook, the preeminent theorist in team productivity. But even though I got a Ph.D. under Dr. Cook's tutelage, I always felt that theories unapplied weren't worth much, so I and two partners started Team StarPath to hone our knowledge and help companies compete.
>
> In the past six years, we've worked with over seventy-two companies, half of which are in the *Fortune* 1000.
>
> I understand you organized into teams a year ago and have had disappointing results. Team StarPath specializes in these kinds of situations. After listening to my talk, I think you'll decide against scrapping the team organization, as I've heard some of you want to do. You'll begin to see ways you can take what you've built thus far and extend the positive results.
>
> Again, we guarantee a productivity increase of 3 percent—based on mutually agreed-upon measures—or you don't pay us. And we can probably get you double that . . .

## The Agile Manager's Checklist

✔ Avoid giving very long presentations or speeches. Few listeners can pay attention beyond forty-five minutes.

✔ If you must give a longer presentation, break it into dissimilar parts.

✔ Don't panic if you're called on to speak without warning. The tricks in this chapter will help you survive.

✔ If called on to speak extemporaneously, ask yourself, "Why am I at this function?" The answer will give you fodder to begin a short speech.

✔ When introducing a speaker, explain to people in the audience: why this speaker, why now, and why to them.

# Index